COPING™

I0811995

COPING WITH TEEN PREGNANCY

Melissa Banigan

Rosen YA™
New York

Published in 2019 by The Rosen Publishing Group, Inc.
29 East 21st Street, New York, NY 10010

First Edition

Library of Congress Cataloging-in-Publication Data

Names: Banigan, Melissa, author.
Title: Coping with teen pregnancy / Melissa Banigan.
Description: New York: Rosen Publishing, 2019 | Series: Coping | Audience: Grades 7–12. | Includes bibliographical references and index.
Identifiers: LCCN 2018017290 | ISBN 9781508183259 (library bound) | ISBN 9781508183242 (pbk.)
Subjects: LCSH: Teenage pregnancy—Juvenile literature. | Teenage parents—Juvenile literature.
Classification: LCC HQ759.4 .B36 2019 | DDC 362.7/8743—dc23
LC record available at https://lccn.loc.gov/2018017290

Manufactured in the United States of America

CONTENTS

INTRODUCTION

What do Aretha Franklin, Whoopi Goldberg, Shirley Temple, and Solange Knowles have in common? Aside from being famous singers and actors, they don't really share much except that they had children when they were teenagers.

According to the Guttmacher Institute, in the United States 44 percent of girls and 49 percent of boys between the ages of fifteen and nineteen years old have had sex. Although only 5 percent of girls in this age group become pregnant, this still equals a whopping 448,000 teenagers per year.

Teenage pregnancy isn't uncommon or abnormal, yet pregnant teenagers often face more difficulties then pregnant adults. In the United States, adolescents are treated as children socially, emotionally, and legally, making it difficult for them to be taken seriously as they try to make decisions about their own reproductive health. In addition, teenagers often have less access to financial resources than adults. This can make it difficult for a teenager who fundamentally disagrees with her family members about how to manage her pregnancy, particularly if she depends on them financially.

The laws that govern teenagers' rights are complicated, and they are often maddening. In the

Teenage pregnancy isn't uncommon or weird. Singer Solange Knowles (sister to Beyoncé) was just one of the hundreds of thousands of people each year who have children as teenagers.

United States, teenagers don't become legal adults until the age of eighteen, but as younger teenagers, they can legally be allowed to drive a car or pilot a plane. Teenagers as young as sixteen can get a passport without parental consent, and seventeen-year-olds can donate blood. In most states, teenagers much younger than eighteen may even receive permission to get married. Teenagers often feel as though they straddle the line between childhood and adulthood.

Regarding a teenager's reproductive health, things get even more confusing. In most states, teenagers under eighteen may place their children for adoption without the permission of their parents or legal guardians, but they must often obtain their permission before getting an abortion, being provided with some forms of birth control, or receiving pain relief when delivering a baby.

Pregnant teenagers will most likely feel a huge range of emotions, including helplessness as they try to understand the complicated laws governing their bodies and their rights.

The first thing pregnant teens need to know is that it is their fundamental human right to choose what to do with their bodies and their pregnancies. Having access to unbiased information about their options, including abortion, adoption, and raising a child, can help teens make the decisions that work for them.

Pregnant teens should also know that support is available for them. In fact, there are many resources, clinics, and agencies to provide help, as well as caring professionals who can offer assistance. Although pregnant teens may feel bewildered by the tangle of laws regarding teenagers and reproductive health, they should keep in mind that they are neither the first nor the last teenagers to be pregnant, and they have the ultimate control over their pregnancies and their futures.

CHAPTER ONE

The Nitty Gritty About Teen Pregnancy

Teenagers have been getting pregnant for as long as humans have existed, yet in today's society, pregnancy and even sexuality among adolescents is stigmatized, making it difficult for many teens to access adequate reproductive health services. Despite the stigma they may face, pregnant teenagers have the right to receive these services, and a pregnancy shouldn't prevent them from growing up to become happy and successful adults.

Teen Pregnancy and Stigma

Despite the large number of adolescents becoming pregnant, American culture stigmatizes teenage

Teenagers are capable of making their own decisions about their bodies and reproductive health. Despite societal stigma, they are not "bad" people if they become pregnant.

pregnancy by pitting "good girls" against "bad girls." This stigma, and the shame it often brings, stems from stereotypes about pregnant teenagers, including that they are irresponsible, promiscuous, and immature. Sadly, there are also plenty of stereotypes about teenagers who choose to become mothers, namely that they will drop out of high school, never go to college, and diminish their chances of success as adults.

Since teenage pregnancy is so common, why is it stigmatized? The answer can be summed up by two words: patriarchy and misogyny. Patriarchy is a social system in which men hold the power. Misogyny means a hatred of women.

Because of the misogyny within patriarchal culture, boys are often considered manly for having sex outside of marriage, while girls are deemed "sluts." Yet becoming pregnant as a teenager isn't inherently bad. It's important to look beyond the stereotypes about teenage parents.

Stereotypes aren't just hurtful; they can also have serious negative long-term effects. In a study published in the *Journal of Research on Adolescence*, Christy Buchanan, a professor of psychology at Wake Forest University, found that teenagers will take greater risks if their parents expect them to fulfill stereotypical roles. Therefore, it's important to not only support teenagers before, during, and after pregnancy but to also trust that they will make good decisions.

Am I Ready to Have Sex?

Some adults will say that people shouldn't have sex before they're married. Others might say they should wait until it feels right. Yet ultimately, it is up to consenting teenagers to decide when they are ready to have sex. Questions to ask partners before sex include the following:

- Do you feel ready to have sex?
- What kind of protection should we use?
- How would you cope if our sex resulted in a pregnancy?
- What makes you feel good?
- Will you tell me if I do something that makes you uncomfortable?

If a teenager feels grossed out by bodies and bodily fluids, it might not be the right time to have sex. Also, if a teen doesn't feel comfortable having a serious conversation with a partner about the literal ins and outs of sex, it might be a good idea to wait a while before having a sexual relationship.

A Teenager's Rights to Reproductive Health Services

According to the United Nations Population Fund (UNFPA), "reproductive rights are human rights." This holds true for all people, whether they are adults, children, or teenagers. Although teenagers under eighteen are often considered by adults to be too immature to deal with big responsibilities, the reality is that they are thoughtful people capable of making important decisions, including about their own reproductive health.

When to See a Doctor

Many teenagers don't feel comfortable speaking with their parents or guardians about sex and pregnancy. They might feel embarrassed or worried about being judged. Some families simply don't provide an environment in which a teen feels safe talking about sex.

Despite not always being able to discuss sex at home, teenagers have the right to have confidential conversations and obtain safe reproductive health services with doctors.

As soon as teenagers start considering becoming sexually active, they should see a doctor to discuss their reproductive health. The same holds true for

Teenagers have the right to have confidential conversations with medical professionals and to receive safe reproductive health services, including birth control, testing for STDs, and abortion.

teenagers who believe they might be pregnant. In fact, all teenagers who have questions about sex, birth control, or pregnancy should speak with a doctor.

Talking about sex might make some teenagers feel squeamish, but responsible, ethical doctors understand that this is largely because of the stigmatization of teenage sex and pregnancy and not because there is anything inherently wrong with teenagers having sex.

Is Talking with a Doctor or Other Professional Confidential?

In the United States, the American Academy of Pediatrics created guidelines that support a teenager's right to reproductive health services without the permission of a parent or guardian. This means that although teenagers living in most states can't legally get a driver's license until the age of sixteen, every state will allow them to receive testing and treatment for sexually transmitted diseases, and many states allow them other reproductive rights, including receiving birth control, pregnancy testing, prenatal care, and abortion services.

Doctors can advise teenagers to speak with their parents about sexuality and pregnancy, but they cannot insist upon it. In fact, doctors can't share any information that their teenage patients give them, unless they feel a teenager is in danger.

Each state has different laws about doctor and teenage patient confidentiality. In New York State, for example, a teenager may receive abortion services without her parents or guardians being notified, whereas in Alabama, she must receive the consent of at least one of her parents.

Teenagers can look up "teenage consent laws by state" on the internet and head to reputable websites such as RAINN, the Guttmacher Institute, and Planned Parenthood to learn about the consent and confidentiality laws in the states where they live.

Affordable Care and Clinics

Many teenagers in the United States have medical insurance under their parents or guardians, and this insurance will often pay for reproductive health services. It's important, however, that teenagers call the 1-800 number on the back of their insurance cards to ask three important questions: 1) What reproductive health services does my insurance cover?; 2) Will bills or other statements about the reproductive health services I receive be sent to my parents or guardians?; and 3) How will my insurance company keep my information confidential?

When a teenager doesn't have health insurance, when her plan doesn't cover reproductive health services, or if bills or statement would be sent to parents or guardians (meaning the services she received wouldn't be confidential), then a great option is to go to Planned Parenthood.

Planned Parenthood's doctors, nurses, and administrative staff support and protect teenagers' confidentiality, and they also assist adolescents in getting the reproductive health services they need, regardless of whether they have insurance. Teenagers can book appointments by looking online for the Planned Parenthood health care center closest to their area, or they can call 1-800-230-PLAN [7526] for more information.

Teen Pregnancy 101

Most teenagers understand, at least in theory, how a person becomes pregnant, yet there's also a lot of misinformation and a general lack of education about the subject.

In the United States, the lowest rates of teenage pregnancy are in the states where teenagers have the most access to reproductive health services and birth control. Therefore, it stands to reason that teenagers should learn about their bodies and reproduction so that they can make more informed choices about sexuality long before they become pregnant.

It's important for pregnant teenagers to visit a doctor. Planned Parenthood is a great health care option for teenagers, regardless of whether they have health insurance.

Sex, Gender, and Pregnancy

Sex and gender are often used interchangeably, but they are actually two different things. A person's sex usually refers to the sexual anatomy with which that person is born. For example, when a baby is born with a penis, he is generally assigned male and raised as a boy. When a baby is born with a vagina, she is typically assigned female and raised as a girl. But people's sexual anatomy doesn't always match their gender identity. Gender identity refers to the gender a person feels themselves to be on the inside.

When it comes to pregnancy, people often assume that only women and girls can become pregnant, and only men and boys can impregnate people, but this is not true. Whether someone has the potential to become pregnant depends on their sex, not their gender. In other words, people with ovaries and a uterus have the potential to become pregnant. These people may be cisgender girls or women, transgender men, or nonbinary or genderqueer individuals. However, when referring to reproductive organs, it is possible to describe people as having male or female anatomy.

Female and Male Sexual Anatomy

Female reproductive organs can be separated into two categories: exterior and interior. The organs that can be seen from the outside of the body, or on the exterior,

Female reproductive system

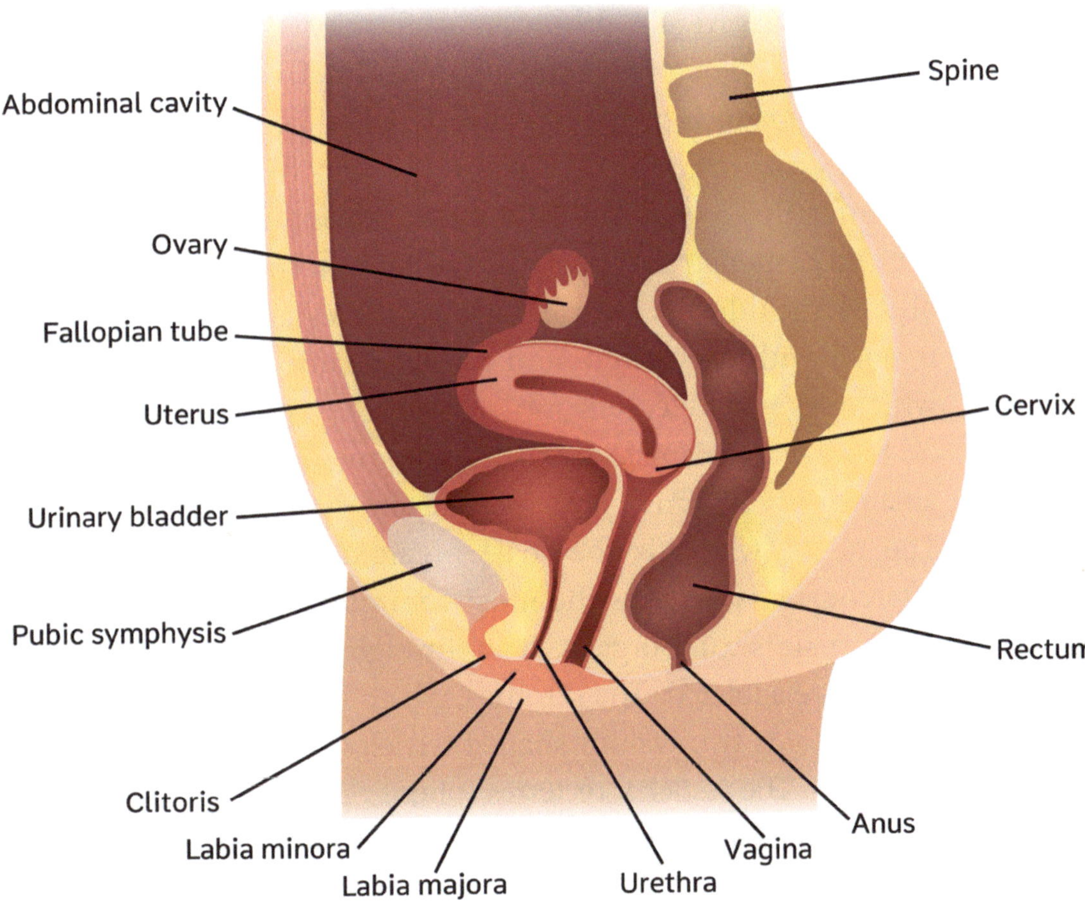

People with female sexual anatomy have both interior and exterior sexual organs. After puberty, these people may get pregnant if they have unprotected vaginal sexual intercourse.

include the vulva (majora and minora), mons pubis, and the clitoris, which is a fascinating sexual organ with no other known purpose than to provide pleasure.

Interior female sexual organs include the vagina, which is a muscular tube that extends from the vulva to the cervix, which, although usually closed, opens to the uterus. The uterus is the organ in which a fertilized egg can grow into a baby inside of a person with female anatomy, and it is also the organ from which an unfertilized egg will be released during a person's monthly menstrual period. Other internal sexual organs include the ovaries, where the eggs a person is born with are stored, and the fallopian tubes, into which eggs are released.

Similar to female sexual anatomy, male sexual anatomy is a system of both internal and external organs. The penis, which is the male organ used for sexual intercourse, is perhaps the most commonly recognized of all male sexual organs. It is through the penis that sperm is ejaculated. The scrotum, which is a sack of skin that contains two walnut-shaped testicles, hangs behind the penis. The testicles, or testes (plural), produce sperm, which is then sent through a system of tubes to the penis.

How Does Someone Get Pregnant?

In order for a pregnancy to occur, one person's sperm must fertilize another person's egg. Though there are a variety of ways this can happen, including doctor-assisted pregnancy, the most common way pregnancy occurs among teenagers is when there has been vaginal sexual intercourse.

Vaginal sexual intercourse is when an erect penis is pushed into a vagina. A person can only become pregnant for a few days out of each month during ovulation, which is the time when an egg is released from one of the ovaries. To become pregnant, an egg must become fertilized by sperm, which is ejaculated by a penis into a vagina.

There are many ways to be romantically or sexually active without the risk of getting pregnant. Kissing alone, for example, can't lead to pregnancy. Nor can anal sex, which is penetration of the anus by a penis or other object, or oral sex, an act in which the genitals of one partner are stimulated by the mouth of the other partner. Only vaginal sexual intercourse (or another method of introducing sperm into the vagina) can lead to a pregnancy.

Birth Control

Teenagers who choose to have vaginal sexual intercourse must consider birth control. Choosing the correct birth control method can feel confusing, particularly because there are so many options. The first step in choosing an effective, safe birth control option is to speak with a doctor or nurse. This is important for a couple of reasons: first, a doctor should always have a teenager's complete medical history before prescribing birth control; second, there's a lot of misinformation out there about birth control, and a doctor can demystify the options and help a teenager choose what's right for her.

Teenagers who aren't comfortable speaking with a family doctor can instead make an appointment at

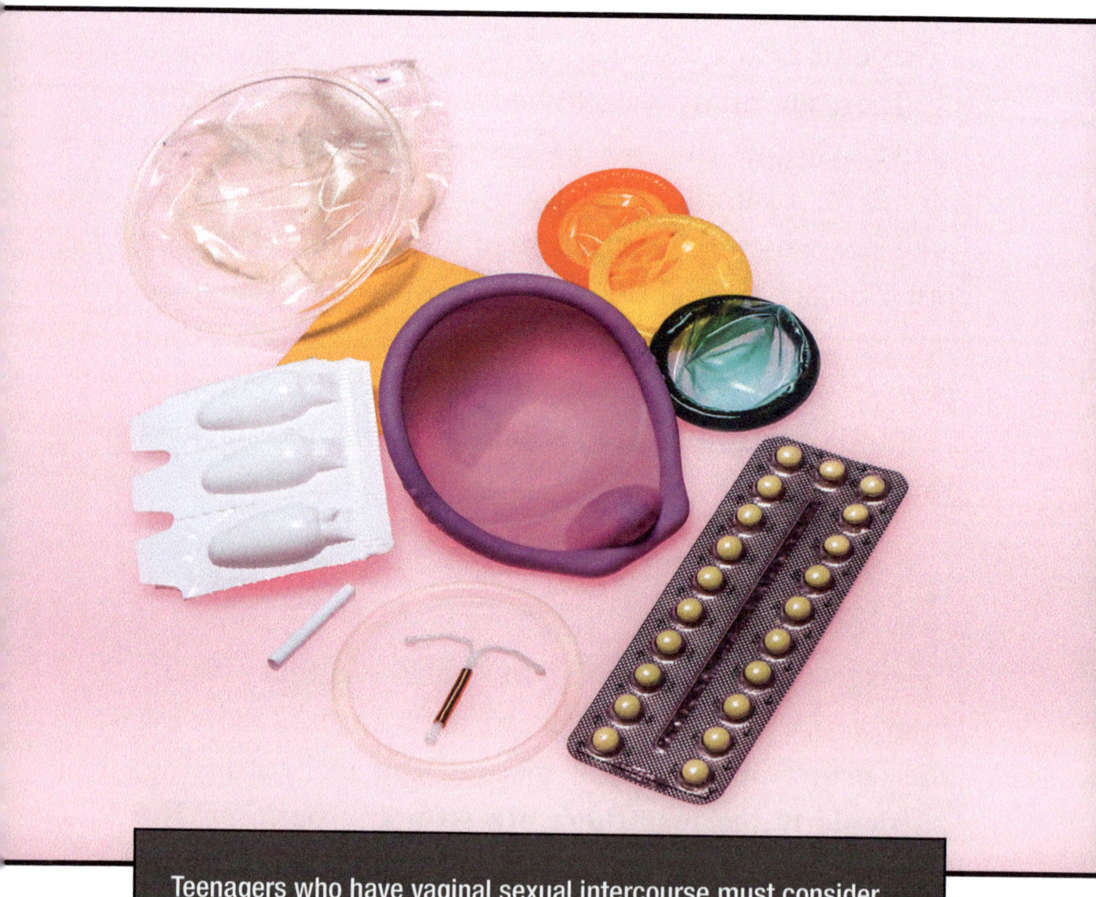

Teenagers who have vaginal sexual intercourse must consider birth control options. A family doctor or other medical professional can help a teenager understand the options.

their local Planned Parenthood, where the doctors and nurses offer judgement-free counseling about birth control options, including birth control pills, implants, patches, shots, sponges, and vaginal rings, as well as IUDs, condoms, cervical caps, abstinence, outercourse (when genitals are rubbed against another person's body without penetration), and the pullout method. Some of these methods are more effective than others.

Before choosing a birth control method, a teenager should first understand how each option works. Some methods, for example, contain hormones, and before using one of them, a teenager should understand potential side effects and risks. Other methods, such as birth control pills, must be taken at the same time every day to be effective.

Abstinence

Abstinence is both the easiest and the most complicated birth control method. Simply explained, abstinence is when a person chooses to not have sex. It's also the only birth control method that is 100 percent effective, because when people don't have vaginal sexual intercourse, sperm can't fertilize an egg to create a pregnancy.

Sounds easy, right? Indeed, abstaining from sex is a great option for many teenagers, and it can be particularly useful for teenagers who believe that sex before marriage is wrong or for those who simply don't want to be in a sexual relationship. Yet it's not always the best birth control method solution.

In twenty-six states, educators are required by law to promote abstinence as the ideal birth control method. Though it sounds great in theory to simply tell teenagers that not having sex is the way to avoid getting pregnant, abstinence-only education actually leads to more pregnancies among teenagers, not fewer.

There have been many scientific studies that show abstinence-only policies fail teenagers. In 2017, the *Journal of Adolescent Health* released a position paper on the topic, stating that abstinence-only government programs in the United States "are ethically flawed, are not evidence-based, and interfere with fundamental human rights to complete and accurate health information."

Teenagers who live in states that stress abstinence-only education but would like more information about other methods of birth control can contact their local Planned Parenthood to learn about other options.

Emergency Contraception

Emergency contraception is a way to prevent pregnancy after having unprotected sex (vaginal sexual intercourse). Sperm can live inside a body for several days after sex, and millions of people use emergency contraception to stop a pregnancy before it starts.

There are four methods of emergency contraception. Only one of them is available over the counter at pharmacies. This option, which has a number of brand names, including Plan B One-Step and Next Choice One Dose, works similarly to a birth control pill in that it delivers hormones to delay ovulation. It may also prevent fertilization of an egg or implantation of a fertilized egg.

Ella, which is prescription only, blocks the hormones that allow a person to conceive. The Yuzpe Method requires a teenager to follow a specific regimen of taking birth control pills that she may already have, although she should contact a doctor for more information. The final and most effective method (99.9 percent) is to have a copper IUD inserted into the uterus by a medical professional. This is the only emergency contraception method that doesn't require hormones, but it does require a visit to a clinic or doctor's office.

A teenager's insurance may cover the cost of emergency contraception, or she may speak with her doctor, pharmacist, or local Planned Parenthood to find out about other payment options.

Myths & FACTS

Myth: Only "bad girls" get pregnant.

Fact: This is perhaps the biggest misconception about teenage pregnancy. No teenager is inherently bad for getting pregnant. However, many teenagers aren't given the information they need in order to deal with the complicated issues surrounding teenage pregnancy.

Myth: A person can't get pregnant the first time she has sex.

Fact: If a teenager has had her first period and has vaginal intercourse without using protection, she most certainly can get pregnant the first time she has sex. Therefore, it's important to use protection every single time you have vaginal intercourse.

Myth: Abstinence-only sexual education prevents teen pregnancy.

Fact: In reality, the states where abstinence-only education is promoted have the highest rates of teen pregnancy, while states that have more comprehensive sexual education have the lowest rates, according to a 2011 study in *PLOS One* journal. When teens have access to the facts, they are better able to make informed decisions and protect themselves and each other.

CHAPTER TWO

What Happens When a Teen Becomes Pregnant?

Teenagers are bound to feel many emotions after they find out that they are pregnant. They may feel scared, worried, sad, excited, happy, or a jumble of emotions all at once. There's no right or wrong way to feel, yet pregnant people will need to navigate these emotions as they quickly consider how they'd like to handle their pregnancies.

How to Know When You Are Pregnant

A missed menstrual period is a sign that a person is pregnant, although a person may still experience spotting (which seems like a very light period) as a fertilized egg and sperm implants itself in the uterine wall.

A teenager may feel a wide range of emotions after a positive pregnancy test. There's no right or wrong way to feel after learning about a pregnancy.

Other signs of pregnancy include feeling more tired than usual, having swollen or tender breasts or sensitive nipples, and experiencing nausea, or feeling ultrasensitive to tastes or smells. Pregnant teenagers may also feel moody or a little dizzy, or they may get headaches.

Most signs of pregnancy are things many teenagers feel regularly, so it's hard to know if they're due to being pregnant. Therefore, it's important for teenagers who suspect they might be pregnant to take a pregnancy test.

Pregnancy tests can be bought from local drug stores. They are usually kept on the shelves and can be purchased from anywhere from a dollar to twenty dollars or so. There is no such thing as a false positive on a pregnancy test. This means that if a test comes back positive, a teenager will want to make an appointment right away to see a doctor. Likewise, if a teenager can't afford a pregnancy test but suspects that she might be pregnant, then she should make an appointment right away to see a medical professional who can give her a test.

What Are the Options?

According to the US Department of Health and Human Services, 77 percent of teen pregnancies are unplanned. No matter the circumstances, it can be very nerve-wracking for teenagers to learn that they are pregnant, particularly as they'll need to make the very important decision about what to do with the pregnancy. These options include having an abortion, carrying a baby to term and placing it for adoption, or giving birth and raising a child. As teens learn more about these choices, there are other important things they'll want to consider, including how to deal with difficult situations at home and at school.

Right to Stay in School

In 1972, Title IX of the Educational Amendments was signed into law, prohibiting discrimination on the basis of sex in schools. Teenagers who become pregnant or who are parents are also covered under this law, and they therefore have the legal right to stay in any and all educational programs, including public and private schools, university, and many extracurricular programs.

To participate in classes and extracurricular activities, a pregnant teenager or teenage parent isn't required to submit a doctor's note, even after giving birth to a child. In addition, pregnant teenagers and teenage parents must be protected against harassment due to their situations. This extends to being protected against name-calling, slut-shaming, or rumors.

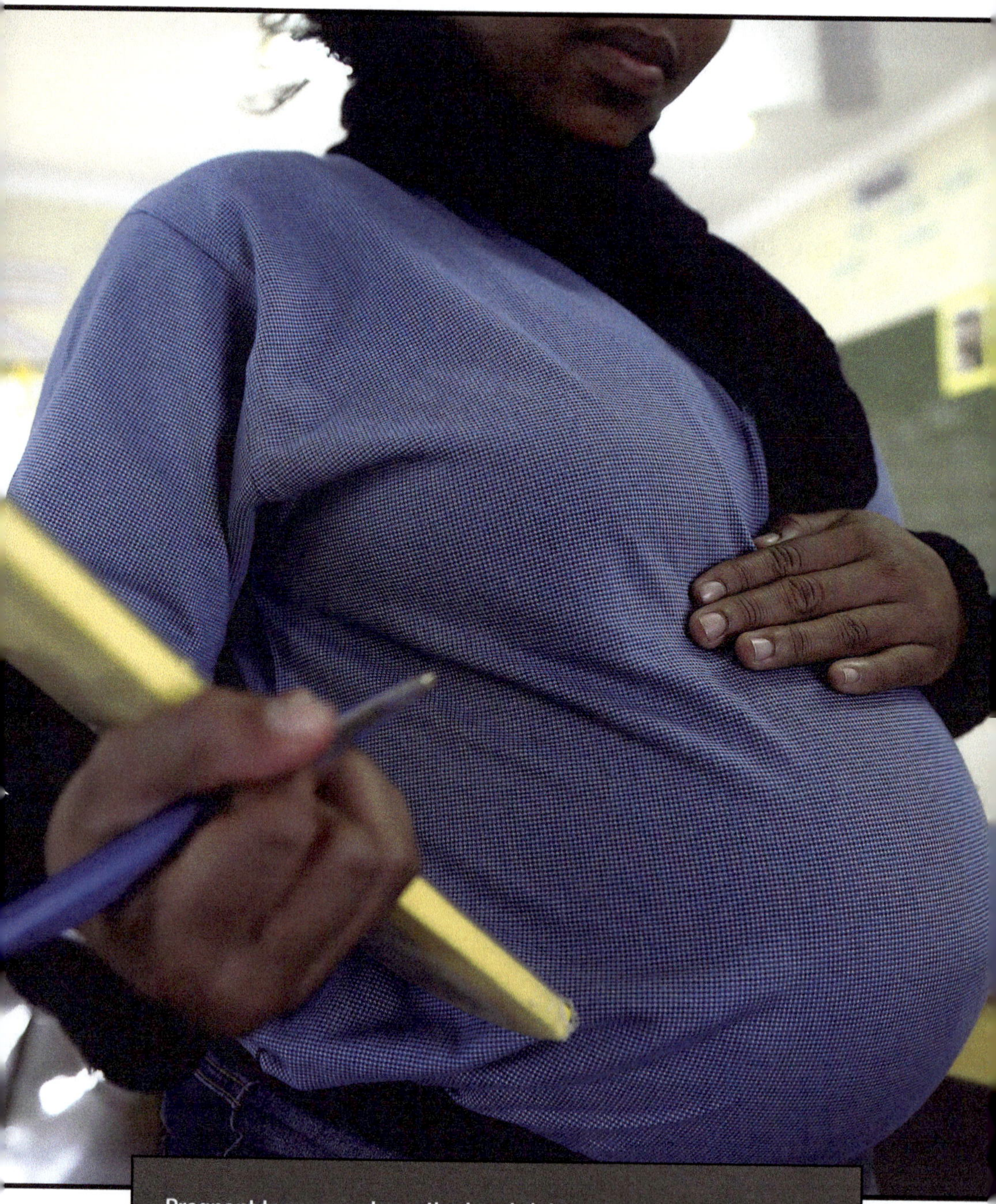

Pregnant teenagers have the legal right to continue attending public and private schools, after-school programs, college, and many extracurricular programs.

If a teenager finds herself being harassed or discriminated against because she is pregnant, has given birth, or has become a parent, she should speak with either a school counselor or Title IX professional. If her school won't address the problem, she may then file a complaint with the Office for Civil Rights at the US Department of Education.

How to Talk with Parents or Guardians

"How will they react?" is probably the biggest question a teenager will wonder when faced with speaking with adults. Just like teenagers, some adults seem cool, calm, and collected when faced with difficulties, while others are quick to feel and express anger.

Most parents and guardians want to be supportive of their teenagers even if they feel disappointed, scared, or sad. They may wonder how a teenager could possibly have gotten into this situation, or they'll feel as though they are personally to blame, but hopefully, they'll also wonder how they can help their teen.

If teenagers feel worried about discussing pregnancy with their parents or guardians, they may decide to speak with doctors, social workers, or nurses about their options.

Teenagers will want to prepare themselves for the conversations they have with adults. It's helpful to write down a list of items to discuss, including whether to have an abortion, adopt out a baby, or raise a child.

Teenagers whose parents or guardians have in the past been violent or seemed out of control, or teens who simply find it difficult to speak with the adults in their lives, can visit a doctor, social worker, nurse, or other professional to talk through their options.

When a Family's Set of Moral Codes Hurts a Teen

Every family lives by its own set of moral codes. Some of these seem simple: be kind to others, be honest, and help out around the house. Other moral codes are more complicated, and they may be influenced by a family's cultural background, religion, and societal gender roles, among many other factors. Many of these moral codes help support and raise children into strong, ethical adults. Others, however, may interfere with pregnant teenagers making the best and healthiest choices for their own bodies and futures.

In many families, for example, teenage pregnancy is stigmatized, and it can be difficult for a teenager to discuss what seems to be a taboo subject. Other families might take a strong political stance against abortion. Pregnant teenagers living in families in which their options seem limited by moral codes might feel confused, ashamed, sad, and even angry over conflicting sets of morals.

In the best circumstances, pregnant teenagers will have the full support of their families. Teenagers who do not feel adequately supported by their families may speak with other trusted adults such as doctors, social workers, or professionals at medical clinics or their local Planned Parenthood.

When Runaway and Homeless Youth Become Pregnant

A study published in the *Journal of Adolescent Health* has indicated that as many as 20 percent of homeless teen girls become pregnant. This is four times higher than other demographics of teenage girls. Being a pregnant teenager can feel especially frightening when one's home life is unstable. Fortunately, there are a number of state, federal, and private programs that can offer assistance, and for teenagers who are still attending school, they can discuss options with social workers. However, some pregnant teenagers no longer attend school. They may instead call the National Runaway Safeline at 800-RUNAWAY to see if there are maternity group homes or transitional living options in their area.

Tips for Talking with Parents and Guardians about Pregnancy

The longer teenagers put off talking with their parents or guardians about their pregnancy, the harder it will become for everyone involved. The easiest way for teenagers to discuss any difficult topic is simply by cutting to the chase and saying something along the lines of, "This is hard for me to say, but I'm pregnant."

Parents or guardians may have strong feelings about which option they'd like for their child to take, and they may even try to pressure teenagers into making a particular decision about how to handle a pregnancy. Therefore, teenagers will want to consider their options before speaking with their parents.

The adults in a pregnant teenager's life may respond to the news with shock or disappointment, or maybe they'll seem completely calm. Having a list of talking points ready to go will help teenagers stay on top of the conversation, no matter how their parents or guardians respond.

What to Do When a Pregnancy Is the Result of Rape

Rape is defined by the FBI as "penetration, no matter how slight, of the vagina or anus with any body part or object, or oral penetration by a sex organ of another person, without the consent of the victim." The legal definition of rape, however, changes state by state.

According to RAINN, girls and young women between the ages of sixteen and nineteen are four times more likely than any other demographic to be victims of rape, attempted rape, or sexual assault. Further, RAINN suggests that every year in the United States, between 7,750 and 12,500 children are conceived from rape.

It is important for pregnant teenage survivors of rape to know that they are not alone, what happened to them wasn't their fault, and that there are options at any

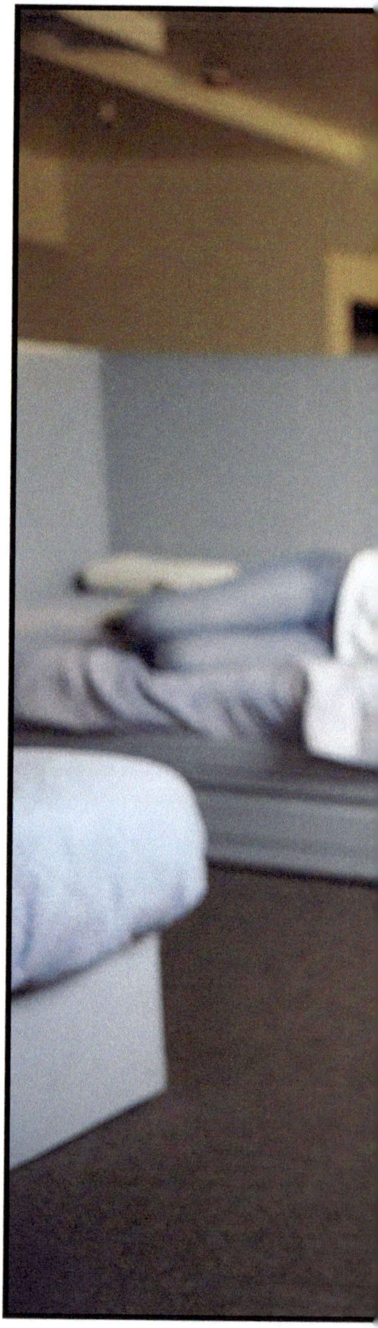

Pregnancy can be particularly frightening for teenagers who are homeless. There are a number of state and federal programs that provide services for teens in this situation.

time during their physical and emotional recovery. Survivors can call the National Sexual Assault Hotline at 1 800-656-HOPE (4673) to speak with a sexual assault service provider in their area who can help them receive care.

Undocumented Immigrant Teens and Pregnancy

There can be additional hurdles for undocumented immigrant teenagers who become pregnant, including being denied abortion services from the Office of Refugee Resettlement, a part of the US Department of Health and Human Services.

Even if a teenager doesn't have legal status in the United States, she still has a constitutional right to reproductive health services, including abortion services. The American Civil Liberties Union (ACLU) has fought lawsuits on behalf of immigrant women, including minors trying to get abortions. To request legal assistance, teenagers can look up their local ACLU chapter via the organization's website: www.aclu.com.

Child Marriage and Teen Pregnancy

Many people think that child marriage is something that only happens to youth living outside of the United States, yet this simply isn't true. The Pew Research Center analyzed data from the Census Bureau's American Community Survey and found that as of 2014, close to 60,000 minors between the ages of fifteen and seventeen were married.

Child marriage is a problem in the United States, but fortunately there are many advocacy groups that work on behalf of teenagers who are married.

Although the age of consent to marriage in all but two states is eighteen, every single state allows for exceptions. In New Hampshire, for example, teens (only girls) as young as thirteen can marry. According to the US Department of Health and Human Services, 11 percent of births to teen girls actually happen inside of marriages.

Pregnant married teenagers can text the AHA Foundation's national crisis hotline for free to connect with professionals who can assist them in things like getting legal assistance or finding emergency shelter. The twenty-four-hour service is anonymous and teenagers can be connected by texting 741-741.

CHAPTER THREE

Abortion

An abortion is a medical procedure that ends a pregnancy. In 2018, the National Academies of Sciences, Engineering, and Medicine determined in a landmark study that abortions are safe and effective. Eighty-eight percent of abortions occur within the first twelve weeks of pregnancy, during the first trimester.

In-Clinic Abortion

The most common type of in-clinic abortion, vacuum aspiration, uses gentle suction to empty a uterus of a pregnancy. Performed by a doctor between five and twelve weeks of a pregnancy, the procedure generally takes between five and fifteen minutes in a clinic.

After a vacuum aspiration, a doctor will examine removed tissue to ensure that the abortion is complete. If it's determined that some tissue from the pregnancy remains in the uterus, then a dilation and curettage (D and C) abortion may also be

When performed during the first trimester of pregnancy, abortion is one of the safest of all medical procedures. It is even safer than getting wisdom teeth removed.

needed. The main difference between vacuum aspiration and dilation and curettage abortions is that the latter procedure requires scraping out the contents of the uterus, rather than sucking, and it can be performed for up to sixteen weeks into a pregnancy.

A study in the journal *PLOS One* showed that 99 percent of American women who have abortions don't regret their decisions, although it was noted that, "Efforts to combat stigma may also support the emotional well-being of women terminating pregnancies." This certainly holds true for teenagers who, after getting an abortion, may feel a variety of emotions, including shame or guilt stemming from the stigmatization of teen pregnancy or abortion in their communities.

Although there are abortion options after the first trimester of pregnancy, they are riskier than the procedures performed early in the pregnancy. Therefore, it's important to speak with a medical professional as early into a pregnancy as possible.

Medication Abortion

Medication abortion, also called the abortion pill, is a two-step method of terminating, or ending, a pregnancy. During the first step, a teenager goes to

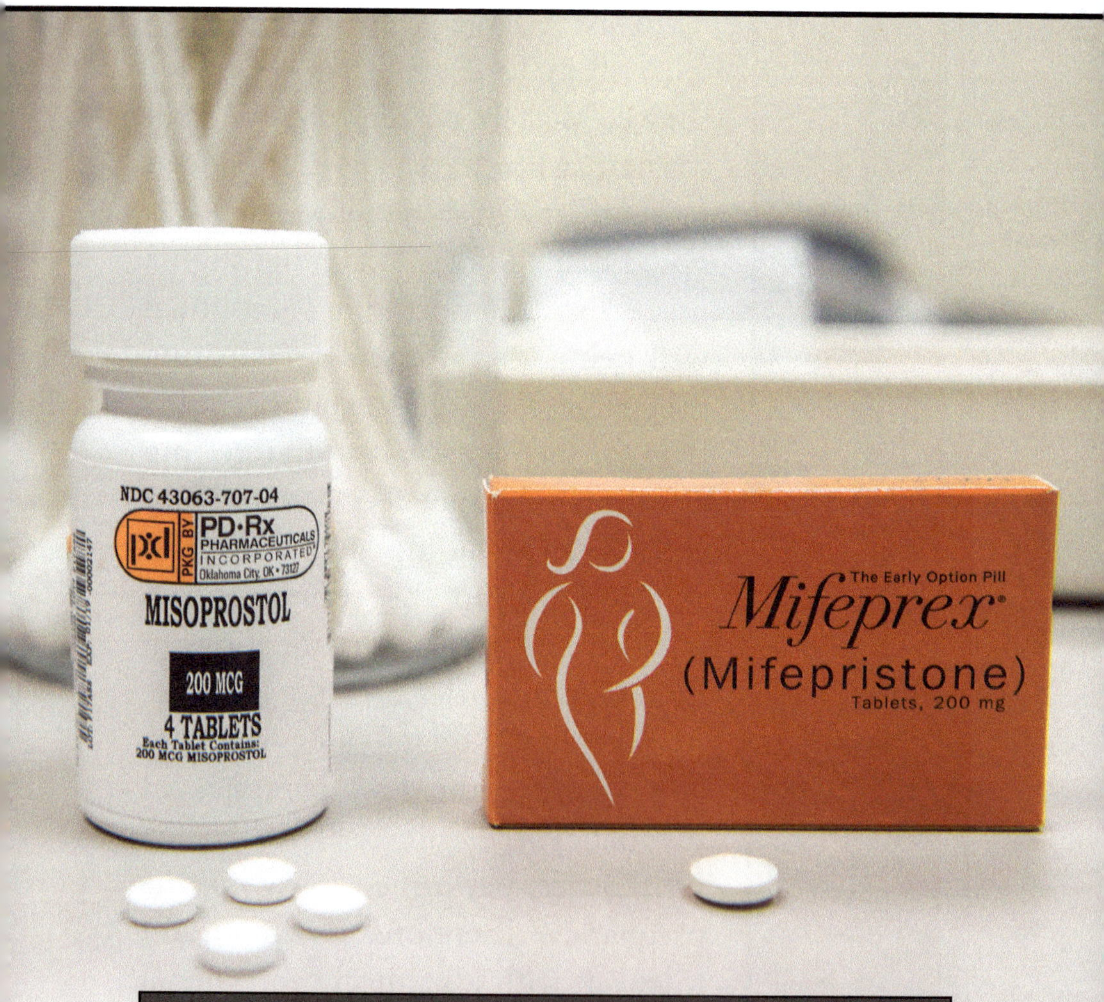

There are two types of abortion: in-clinic abortion and medication abortion. The drugs mifepristone and misoprostol are used for medication abortion.

a clinic and takes a pill called mifepristone. This pill blocks the body from producing progesterone, a hormone needed to maintain a pregnancy.

During the second step, another pill is taken at home. This medicine, called misoprostol, causes bleeding and cramping, causing the uterus to expel a pregnancy.

Choosing whether to have an in-clinic abortion or a medication abortion is a personal decision. Some people prefer an in-clinic abortion because they want a doctor and other medical staff to be there for every part of the procedure. Others prefer a medication abortion because, although the procedure still involves an initial visit to a clinic, most of the processes of the abortion happen at home, and there's no need for surgery or anesthetic.

Although people can get an in-clinic abortion up to thirteen weeks into their pregnancies, they can only get a medication abortion up to ten weeks.

Is Abortion Safe?

When an abortion is performed during the first trimester of pregnancy, it is one of the safest of all medical procedures. According to a 2012 study in *Obstetrics & Gynecology* comparing childbirth and legally obtained abortion, there were only 0.6 deaths for every 100,000 abortions (compared to 8.8 deaths per the same number of live births). In fact, in a 2015 study in the same publication, a person is less likely to have complications from having an abortion than from having her wisdom teeth removed!

Although there aren't usually any serious long-term physical or emotional side effects associated with having an abortion, as with any medical procedure, complications can occur. For example, a person could experience an allergic reaction to one of the medications she receives, or she might have an incomplete abortion, which is when a small amount of pregnancy tissue remains inside her uterus.

Doctors who perform abortions provide their patients with aftercare instructions, including a list of potentially serious symptoms. Although serious complications from having an abortion are rare, teenagers should follow all the aftercare instructions they receive and contact their clinic or doctor's office with any questions.

Parental Consent and Notification

In most states, there are laws that require parents or guardians to either be notified or give their consent before their teenager under the age of eighteen gets an abortion. Parental notification is required prior to an abortion in thirty-seven states, while parental consent must be given in twenty-one states.

Why Abortion Is About More Than Health Care

At eighteen years old, Kim Jorgensen Gane felt relieved after getting an abortion, and she was thankful for the doctor and other health care professionals who assisted her with the procedure. "The year after my procedure," she told the author, "the same clinic in Kalamazoo, Michigan, was firebombed by anti-abortion terrorists."

The clinic soon moved to a temporary location so that it could continue providing reproductive services, and today, as an adult, Jorgensen Gane is more appreciative than ever for the services she received as a teenager. Jorgensen Gane says:

> Abortion is a highly politicized topic, and yes, it's about a woman's right to choose, but ultimately it's an economic issue. Access to birth control and abortion care is about prioritizing the lives of women and children. Women deciding for themselves when and whether to have children is about more than healthcare, it's about education, opportunity, pay equity, family leave, and other issues that are traditionally considered "women's issues"—issues that overwhelmingly keep women and children in poverty. But when women prosper, their families prosper. Period.

Although the majority of states require some level of parental involvement before a teenager can get an abortion, all states allow teenagers autonomy over their decisions to carry babies to term, give birth, and place their children for adoption.

It's a good idea for all teens to learn about the legislation around parental consent and notification in their state. Planned Parenthood can always assist teenagers by giving them unbiased information about the laws in their state and discussing all of the options.

Judicial Bypass

Sometimes, a teenager may disagree with her parents or guardians about the best choice regarding her pregnancy. In 1972, the US Supreme Court ruled that states can't give parents absolute power over their child's decision to have an abortion. Therefore, most states now offer an option for teens who don't want to be forced to either receive their parents' consent or have their guardians be notified. This option, called judicial bypass, includes a teenager receiving permission from a court, rather than parents, to have an abortion.

Laws vary in each state, but they generally involve a judge assessing a teenager's emotional maturity, ability to understand abortion procedures and recovery, and ability to make responsible decisions. Judges' power over teenagers is often subjective. In some cases their

In 1973, the US Supreme Court decided, in a case called *Roe v. Wade*, that abortion is a fundamental right under the Constitution. To this day, abortion remains a political topic.

decisions may be based on their political beliefs rather than what's best for teenagers.

Although judicial bypass is a legal alternative for teens to obtain adoptions without parental involvement, it's important to note that judges, like parents, are not medical professionals. In fact, many medical groups oppose parental involvement altogether, including the American Academy of Pediatrics, the Society for Adolescent Medicine, and the American College of Obstetricians and Gynecologists.

The Politics of Abortion

No other option for pregnant people is more politicized than abortion, and the complicated issues surrounding the procedure can be very confusing. Pregnant teenagers may find it helpful to have a better understanding of the history of abortion as they make their own decisions.

Roe v. Wade and Pro-Choice versus Pro-Life

In 1973, the US Supreme Court announced its decision in a case called *Roe v. Wade*, saying that abortion was a fundamental right under the Constitution. In addition, the Court decided that a previously established clause in the Fourteenth Amendment granting the right to privacy was "broad enough to encompass a woman's decision whether or not to terminate her pregnancy."

Despite the decision made by the US Supreme Court, abortion remains a highly politicized issue in America. There are people on one side of the fence who support the Court's decision. These people, called pro-choice advocates, believe that women should have the

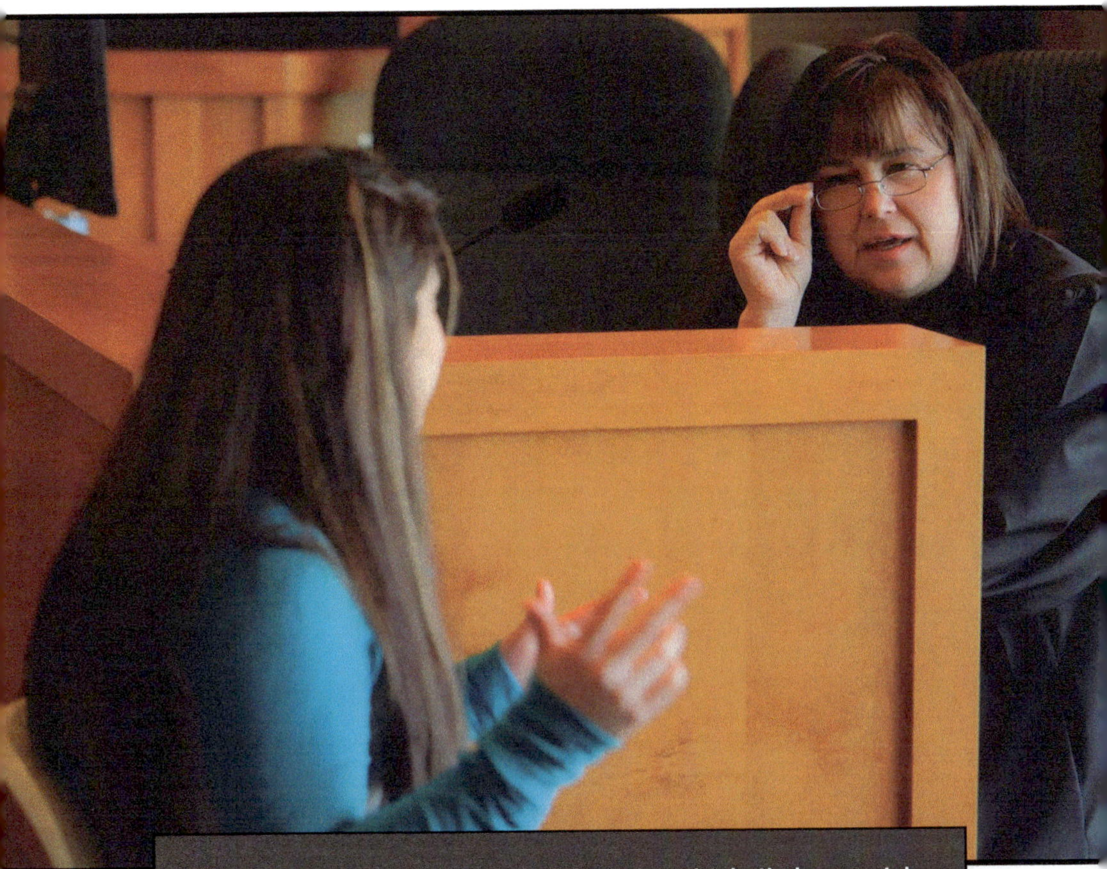

Teenagers who don't want to be forced to obtain their parents' consent or have their guardians be notified about an abortion can try to get a judicial bypass.

right to choose what's best for their bodies, including whether to get an abortion. On the other side of the fence sit people who are called pro-life advocates. These individuals believe in giving rights to an embryo or fetus rather than to the pregnant person, and they say that abortion is murder.

Checklist for Getting Judicial Bypass

Some teenagers won't want to tell their parents about their pregnancies, and despite laws in many states saying they must, the US Supreme Court has offered an alternative route, called judicial bypass. The steps for getting a waiver to get an abortion from a judge include the following:

- Calling a teenager's local Planned Parenthood to find out the parental consent and notification laws in her state as well as the process for getting a judicial bypass.
- Setting up a date for a hearing with a judge.
- Getting a lawyer to assist with the process. Lawyers are appointed by the court and their services are free.
- Showing up to the private hearing and answering all of the judge's questions. A teenager will want to be prepared with answers to questions such as, "Why do you want to get an abortion?" "Why aren't you telling your parents?" and "Do you understand the process of getting an abortion?"

In short, based on a brief hearing, a judge will then need to make a decision about a teenager's maturity. Therefore, it's important that teenagers present themselves with maturity as they explain why getting an abortion is in their best interests. In most states, a judge will then have up to a few days to come to a decision.

A pregnant teenager may feel confused by the politicizing of abortion, particularly if she's bombarded with differing views from both pro-choice and pro-life advocates. Yet at the end of the day, the laws of the land say that no matter what her personal views are about abortion, a teenager is ultimately able to choose whether she herself decides to get one.

Hyde Amendment

Many teenagers, particularly those living in conservative states with fewer reproductive health resources, cannot easily pay for their abortions. The Hyde Amendment, which is a law preventing federal funds from paying for abortion except under special circumstances, makes this even more difficult, particularly for low-income pregnant people.

Since 1976, the Hyde Amendment has even prevented Medicaid from paying for abortion services unless a pregnancy would endanger the pregnant person's life or if a pregnancy is the result of incest or rape. When insurance isn't allowed to pay for an abortion, teenagers must then come up with the cash, carry their pregnancy to term, or find other avenues of support through organizations such as Planned Parenthood. Additionally, although the Hyde Amendment prohibits federal funds from paying for abortions, many states use their own funds to pay for the procedure.

Supporters of the Hyde Amendment see it as a method of limiting the number of people who obtain abortions. Yet systemic racism in the United States means that low-income women of color form the majority of people enrolled in Medicaid, which means that they are most often the ones denied federal payment for abortion services.

Those in opposition to the amendment believe that, similarly to parental consent and notification laws, the Hyde Amendment stands in the way of letting a pregnant person make her own private reproductive health decisions with her doctor.

CHAPTER FOUR

Raising a Child

Deciding to have and raise a child is a life-altering experience for any person, particularly for a teenager just approaching adulthood. Once a person makes the decision to have a baby (rather than place a baby for adoption or obtain an abortion), she must then consider prenatal care. She'll also need to plan for all the things she'll need to help welcome a baby into the world.

Ready to Become a Parent?

Before teenagers decide to have a baby, they need to carefully consider whether they are actually ready to become parents. Raising a child can be a deeply rewarding experience, but it involves much more than rocking a cute baby to sleep, and it requires a high level of maturity and lifelong commitment.

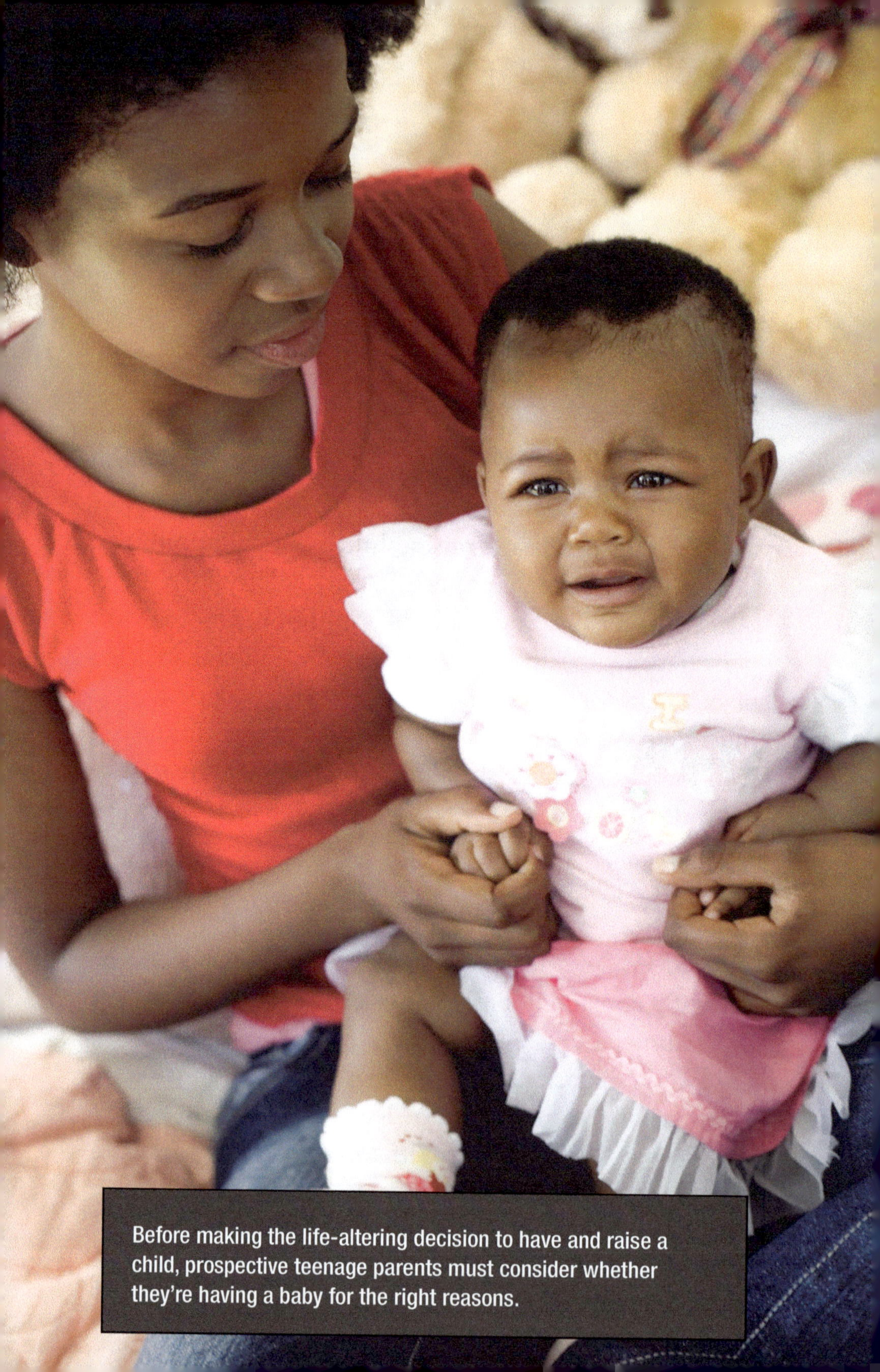

Before making the life-altering decision to have and raise a child, prospective teenage parents must consider whether they're having a baby for the right reasons.

Teenagers should think about whether a baby would want them as his or her parent. Questions they might want to ask themselves include: Am I in a position to provide a stable home for a baby? Will having a child prohibit me from following my dreams? Am I ready to deal with whatever parenting throws my way, including illnesses, long crying sessions, being sleep deprived, and visits to the doctor?

Above all else, prospective teenage parents should ask themselves if they're considering having a baby for the right reasons. It's never a good idea to have a baby in order to save a relationship, or as a way to make someone fall in love with you.

Prenatal Care

Although most of the hard work of raising a child happens after a person has given birth, it's also vital to receive prenatal care. This means regular visits to a health care provider who helps monitor the health of both the pregnant person and the unborn baby.

Where and How to Find a Health Care Provider

Finding a great health care provider is the first step to receiving proper prenatal care. Some teenagers still see pediatricians, and others might not ever have seen a gynecologist. Pregnant teenagers will want to make an appointment with a doctor or nurse who specializes in treating pregnant people and babies. The names for some of these professionals include obstetricians and midwives. Teenagers may speak with their primary physicians or pediatricians about their pregnancies, and they may receive referrals to other medical providers. Teenagers who don't regularly see a doctor or who don't have health insurance can make an appointment at their local Planned Parenthood, which is an organization that doesn't deny care based on a lack of income.

Medicaid and Health Insurance

It costs a lot of money to have a baby, and doctor bills and hospital fees add up quickly. Therefore, it's important for a pregnant teenager to consider how she's going to pay for her prenatal care, labor and delivery, and postpartum care (also called

Medical bills and other costs related to having a baby can quickly add up. However, keep in mind that you may not really need all the baby gear that is advertised to new parents.

aftercare). If a teenager is on a health insurance plan, she will want to call the 1-800 number on the back of her health card to find out what is covered. If she's not yet on insurance, she can either speak with Planned Parenthood to learn about her options or she can sign up for Medicaid.

Jointly funded by the federal government and states, Medicaid programs pay for a large percentage of the medical costs associated with pregnancy, childbirth, and postpartum care. Teenagers living on their own may, depending on the state in which they live, apply for Medicaid without the assistance of an adult. Some states, however, require an adult to help a minor apply.

The Women, Infants, and Children (WIC) Program

It's important for people to have access to good nutrition while they are pregnant. The Women, Infants, and Children (WIC) program helps many pregnant people receive healthy food to supplement their existing diet while they're pregnant, and they and their babies may also receive additional food after the birth.

To learn more about whether they may receive assistance from WIC, pregnant teenagers can ask their doctors for information or they may reach out directly to the US Department of Agriculture Food and Nutrition Service, which is the government agency responsible for administering the program.

What to Expect Physically

During a pregnancy, a teenager's body will change drastically due to hormones coursing through her system. During the first few months of pregnancy, which is called the first trimester, pregnant people may feel more tired than usual, their breasts may grow and become sore, and they may feel nauseous (this is called morning sickness), have an increased urge to urinate, have acne, or feel more emotional than usual. Other teenagers may not feel many physical or emotional symptoms.

During the second and third trimesters (which are approximately three months each), teenagers will start to see more pronounced changes. Their waistlines will expand as their bellies and uteruses grow, and they may find that they gain weight or that their feet and ankles swell. In addition, they may see a darkening in skin tone on some areas of their bodies.

Many teenagers feel self-conscious about their bodies. Teenagers may feel upset as they see their bodies go through so many drastic changes, but they should be assured that, unless a doctor tells them otherwise, what is happening is normal and natural.

Both parents are legally responsible for providing for their child. Child support is an ongoing financial payment made by one parent to another parent to pay for necessities for a child.

Teenagers may also want to embrace these bodily changes as remarkable. After all, they are the result of the creation of an entire new human.

Responsibilities of the Partner

There is an enormous lack of programming and support for teenage partners of pregnant people. This is largely because of the system of patriarchy, which has built the false belief that mothers are more nurturing than fathers. Teenage fathers should know, however, that although the decision of whether to have a child isn't up to them (as it is always up to the individual who is pregnant), they not only have parental rights and responsibilities but they are also just as capable of being as loving and nurturing a parent as a mother.

Voluntary Acknowledgment of Paternity

An Acknowledgment of Paternity is a document signed by both unmarried parents to legally establish their baby's legal father. The document, signed after the birth of a baby, is as powerful as a court order determining a child's legal father, and it establishes that both parents must support their baby.

A teenager will want to consider signing an Acknowledgment of Paternity if he believes he is the parent because it gives him certain parental rights. For example, even if he isn't in a relationship with the baby's mother, he may have custody and visitation rights, and his consent would likely be needed before the child could be given up for adoption. Legally acknowledging his paternity will also mean that he may be required to pay child support.

Court Petitions and Genetic Testing

When a teenager doubts that he is the parent, either he or the mother may file a petition to have a court determine his paternity. Usually, the court will order the father, mother, and baby to provide genetic tests that definitively show whether the child and alleged father are biologically related. If they are related, then the court will determine him the legal father, which could mean he is responsible for child support and has custody or visitation rights.

Child Support

Legally, both parents have a responsibility to provide for their child. Child support is an ongoing monthly financial payment made by one parent to another parent that helps ensure a child has a place to live, food, and any other necessities. It can be used for school fees, extra-curricular activities, medical expenses, and

There are a number of organizations that provide services to teen parents, especially single mothers. You may be able to get free diapers and other baby supplies.

other costs that directly benefit the child. Although child support isn't paid until after a baby is born, it's a good idea for a prospective father to consider his responsibilities well before he is required to jump into the fray.

Becoming a Single Mother

Just as there is a stigma against teenage mothers, there is also a cultural stigma against single mothers. This is largely because, in a patriarchal society, single women are often viewed as "sinners" for having sex outside of marriage, and they are considered unfit parents if they aren't part of a "traditional" two-parent home that contained both a mother and a father. Yet there is nothing inherently bad about becoming a single mother, and in fact, it happens regularly. In just the United States, there are nearly 14 million single parents, the majority of whom are single mothers.

Despite single parenthood families being just as normal as two-parent families, raising a child alone is tough, especially with the attached stigmas. Therefore, single mothers may want to tap into programs within their communities for support. Often run by the state, these programs may include assistance with school or preparations for the high school equivalency test to obtain their General Educational Development (GED). Other programs assist with social and health services, and still other programs help new teenage mothers with child care.

CHAPTER FIVE

Adoption

In the early and mid-twentieth century, when there was even more stigma against single mothers, most teenage girls who gave birth put their babies up for adoption. Today, according to the National Committee for Adoption, only two to three out of every one hundred teenage pregnancies lead to adoptions. Most states allow teenage mothers to give their children up for adoption without the involvement or consent of their parents.

Choosing Adoption

In today's society, teenagers are still viewed and treated as children, and they may not feel emotionally ready to become parents. In addition, they may not be in a position to provide financially for a child or they may want to finish school or reach other milestones before starting a family.

Only two to three out of every one hundred teenage pregnancies lead to adoptions. Adoption means giving birth to a baby who will then be raised by another family.

If a pregnant teenager decides that she isn't yet ready to become a parent, then she has two options: abortion or adoption. Abortion will terminate a pregnancy, while adoption will allow the pregnant person to carry the baby to term, give birth, and then place the baby with a family, couple, or individual adult who will become the baby's legal parent or parents.

Placing a baby for adoption can be a great gift for a family that might not be able to conceive a child, and it is, in large part, a selfless decision. A pregnant teenager should think carefully, however, before moving ahead with this option. First, she should ask herself if this is really the decision she wants to make, or if she's being influenced by the moral or religious values of her family, community, school officials, or partner. If she's feeling forced to carry a baby to term, she should discuss her feelings, personal desires, and options with a social worker or medical provider at either a clinic or her local Planned Parenthood.

In addition, a pregnant teenager considering adoption should know that carrying a baby to term and giving birth is more dangerous than getting an abortion. In the abstract to a study comparing the safety of abortion and childbirth published in *Obstetrics & Gynecology*, Elizabeth Raymond and David Grimes wrote, "Legal induced abortion is markedly safer than childbirth. The risk of death associated with childbirth is approximately 14 times higher than that with abortion."

A teenager should think about how she'll feel carrying a child to term. As her body changes and starts showing the signs of a pregnancy, how might she feel at school or in her community? Does she believe she'll feel supported, or does she fear being stigmatized? Can she commit to healthy habits during her entire pregnancy and go regularly to a doctor to receive prenatal care?

Finally, a teenager should carefully consider how she might feel giving birth to a child that will then be raised by another family. The feelings surrounding adoption are complicated. Therefore, a pregnant teen considering this option should speak with social workers and other trusted adults before she makes a final decision. No matter what, a pregnant teenager should know that even if she places her child for adoption into another family, she will always be that child's birth mother, and no one, not ever, can take that away from her.

Adoption Arrangements

After a teenager makes the decision to place her child for adoption, she has a couple important options to consider. In decades past, most adoptions were closed, which meant that

It's more common to have an open rather than a closed adoption. An open adoption means that a birth mother and the adoptive parents stay in contact.

after a birth parent gave birth, she could no longer have contact with her child or the adoptive parents. Today, it's much more common to have an open adoption, in which birth parents and adoptive parents remain in contact. Choosing whether to have a closed or open adoption is a personal decision, although teenagers should know that most adoption agencies support only open adoptions, as there's a general belief that closed adoptions aren't good for a child's well-being.

Closed versus Open Adoptions

There are pros and cons to both closed and open adoptions. A closed adoption may help some birth parents feel better able to close the door on what might have been a painful chapter of their lives. This option, also called "confidential" or "secret" adoption, involves the records of the birth parent being sealed by a court. These sealed records allow a birth parent to remain unknown. However, various organizations help adopted people locate their birth mothers, and there's ultimately no guarantee that records will remain sealed forever.

In the United States, most domestic adoptions are open, which means that adopted children benefit from having a relationship with their birth parents. Open adoptions can take shape in many ways. Some arrangements allow adoptive parents and birth parents to have contact through lawyers, while other arrangements promote strong relationships between both families, even letting them meet in person.

Sometimes, however, children living in open adoption situations suffer if they've formed a relationship with a birth parent who either disappears or stops calling. A birth parent may drop out of the picture for many reasons. Some birth parents might feel shame, guilt, or sadness when they see the children they birthed being raised by another family. Others might have other issues that keep them away.

Once a teenager makes a decision to put her child up for adoption, she must realize that,although her priority should be ensuring her child's needs are met, she needs to also focus on her emotional and physical well-being. Speaking with social workers and adoption counselors at an adoption agency about her options will help a pregnant teenager decide between a closed or open adoption. Note, however, that closed adoption is not the preferred option of most social workers and adoption agencies, as it often isn't in the best interest of the child.

Coming Up with an Adoption Plan

As most domestic adoptions are open, teenagers have a few big choices to make regarding the placement of their children. First, they'll want to choose an adoption agency. They may do this by asking a social worker or doctor for advice, or they may want to contact the Children's Bureau, which is an Office of the Administration for Children and Families at the US Department of Health and Human Services.

Once a teenager finds the adoption agency with which she would like to work, she should know that the first step in placing her child for adoption is to legally terminate her rights as a parent. This is a permanent decision, meaning that it cannot be reversed. Therefore, a pregnant person must be absolutely certain before beginning the process that this is what she wants. Depending on the state in which she lives, there is, however, a short period of time when she can revoke her consent, or change her mind about terminating her parental rights.

Depending on the adoption agency with which a teenager chooses to work, part of coming up with an adoption plan involves choosing an adoptive family for the child. Birth parents may also choose what kind of contact they want to have with the adopted family and the child. Perhaps they only want an annual update,

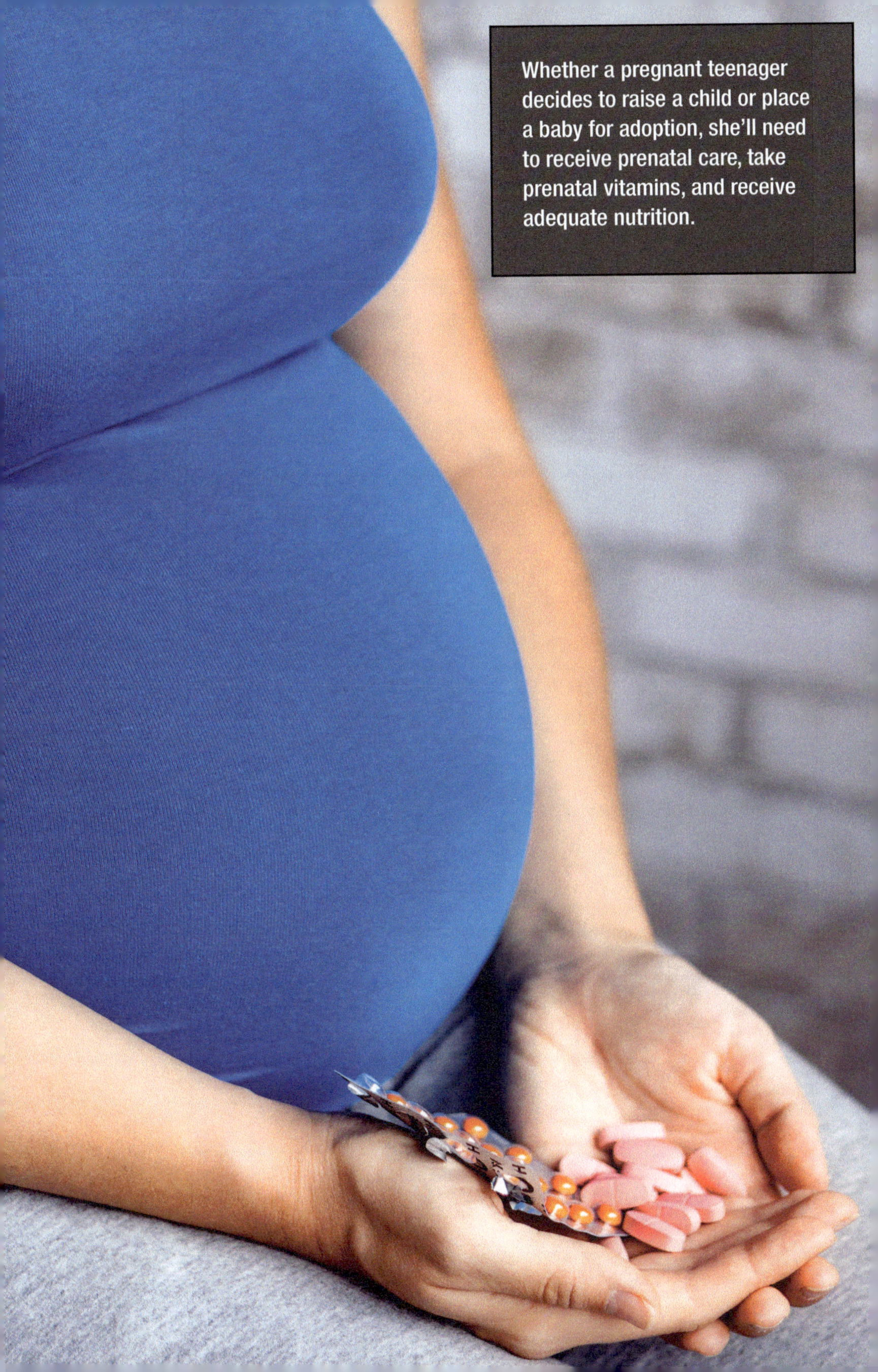

Whether a pregnant teenager decides to raise a child or place a baby for adoption, she'll need to receive prenatal care, take prenatal vitamins, and receive adequate nutrition.

or maybe they'd prefer to meet monthly to form a relationship. Adoption agencies can help find families who are comfortable with the same sort of arrangement as the birth parent.

After teenagers have developed an adoption plan and chosen families to raise their children, they'll want to regularly receive prenatal care from a doctor. They will need to take prenatal vitamins and receive adequate nutrition to ensure their growing children are healthy. For the duration of their pregnancies, pregnant people will want to refrain from unhealthy habits such as smoking, drinking alcohol, and doing other drugs.

What Happens After the Baby Is Born?

Teenagers may feel a lot of anxiety not only over childbirth but also about what will happen in the hours and days after their babies are born. They may decide to let the adoptive parents witness the birth, or they may not. Also, they may decide to see their children, or they may not. Often, the adoptive parents will take the children directly home from the hospital or other birth setting.

A birth parent can name her baby before terminating her parental rights. This name will appear on the child's birth certificate. Although adoptive parents can

Teenagers may feel a wide range of emotions after placing a baby for adoption, and it's important that all of their feelings be honored.

rename the child, they will often discuss this with the birth mother and come up with a compromise that reflects all of the parents' interests.

If a teenager hasn't already terminated her parental rights during her pregnancy, she'll be asked to give her consent to the adoption after the birth of her child.

Teenagers who have just given birth may feel emotionally drained. They may feel despair over their decision to place their children for adoption, or they may feel relief. They may feel a number of emotions all at once. All of their feelings should be honored, and they should be provided with access to social workers and counselors to help them deal with what they're going through. Teenagers should know that they don't need to quickly "get over it." They may feel emotionally fine following the birth, but months or years down the line they may find they need to speak with a therapist for support.

Teenagers who have just given birth will also need time to physically recover. They will most likely feel some discomfort, and their breasts may feel painful as their milk comes in. It is important for them to carefully follow their doctor's aftercare advice and give themselves plenty of time to recover.

CHAPTER SIX

Childbirth

No matter how you look at it, giving birth to a baby is a big deal. Teenagers should speak not only with their doctors about what will happen during labor and delivery but they should also talk with their parents or guardians, social workers, and other trusted adults about what to expect after the babies are born.

What Happens During Birth?

The thought of giving birth to a child might fill a teenager with anxiety. Movies depicting screaming women as they give birth don't help, nor does the media, which teaches us that childbirth is just plain awful. In reality, everyone's experience of childbirth is different.

Childbirth is really two separate processes: labor and delivery. It is the ending of a pregnancy, involving a baby leaving its parent either through her uterus and vaginal passage or by cesarean

Pregnant teenagers should speak with their doctors about what to expect during labor and delivery, as well as with trusted adults about what to expect after the baby is born.

section (C-section), which is a surgical delivery via the parent's abdomen.

If she's having a vaginal birth, a teenage parent has a lot of control over the process. In regard to pain management, she can decide whether she prefers nonpharmaceutical relief, pharmaceutical medications, or a combination of both. She can choose where she wants to have her baby and whom she wants to be involved in the birth.

If it appears that a teenage mother will need a C-section, she still has a lot of control over what will happen to her body, although she'll want to discuss the process with her doctor ahead of the delivery.

Doctors, Midwives, and Doulas

In the United States, most pregnant people see an obstetrician-gynecologist (OB/GYN) for prenatal care and delivery. This doctor specializes in providing care to people during pregnancy, childbirth, and in all other manner of reproductive health.

For thousands of years, however, midwives and doulas have also helped people give birth. Midwives attend to the medical needs of a labor and birth, and they are concerned with the health of a mother and child. A certified nurse midwife (CNM) has training as both a traditional nurse and a midwife, while a certified midwife (CM) is a midwife, but not a nurse.

A doula, on the other hand, attends more to the emotional needs of a pregnant person. She will typically meet with a pregnant person (and potentially her partner, too) well before the due date to discuss the expectations for childbirth, and she will act as an advocate for the pregnant person throughout her labor and delivery.

Pregnant teenagers have a right to choose who provides their care, although they will want to check with their insurance companies to see what will be covered. It is typical, for example, for an OB/GYN to be covered by insurance and less typical for a midwife's or doula's services to be covered. Teenagers may, however, reach out to organizations such as Radical Doula to learn about volunteer doula services in their area, and they should speak with their doctors or social workers about finding a midwife.

Birth Plan

It seems easy: a person goes into labor, and voila, out pops a baby. In reality, every labor and birth is different, and teenagers should make a birth plan that details all of their hopes for the birth. Do they want to have an epidural to provide pain relief, or would they like to have massages and acupuncture instead, if possible? Do they want their partner or parents to witness the birth, or, if they're placing the child for adoption, do they want the adoptive parents to be on hand? Pregnant teenagers should speak with their OB/GYNs, midwives, or doulas to discuss all of the options available to them.

It is important to note that birth does not always go according to how one plans it. People may plan to go without medication for pain relief, but they may change their minds during labor and decide that they do need an epidural after all. Also, sometimes medical complications mean that it is necessary to deliver via cesarean section, even if this contradicts the person's birth plan. So, when planning a birth, pregnant people should know what they want, but they should also be prepared to be flexible.

A teenager's birth plan shouldn't leave out what happens after the delivery. For example, if she has decided to exclusively breastfeed, then she'll want to

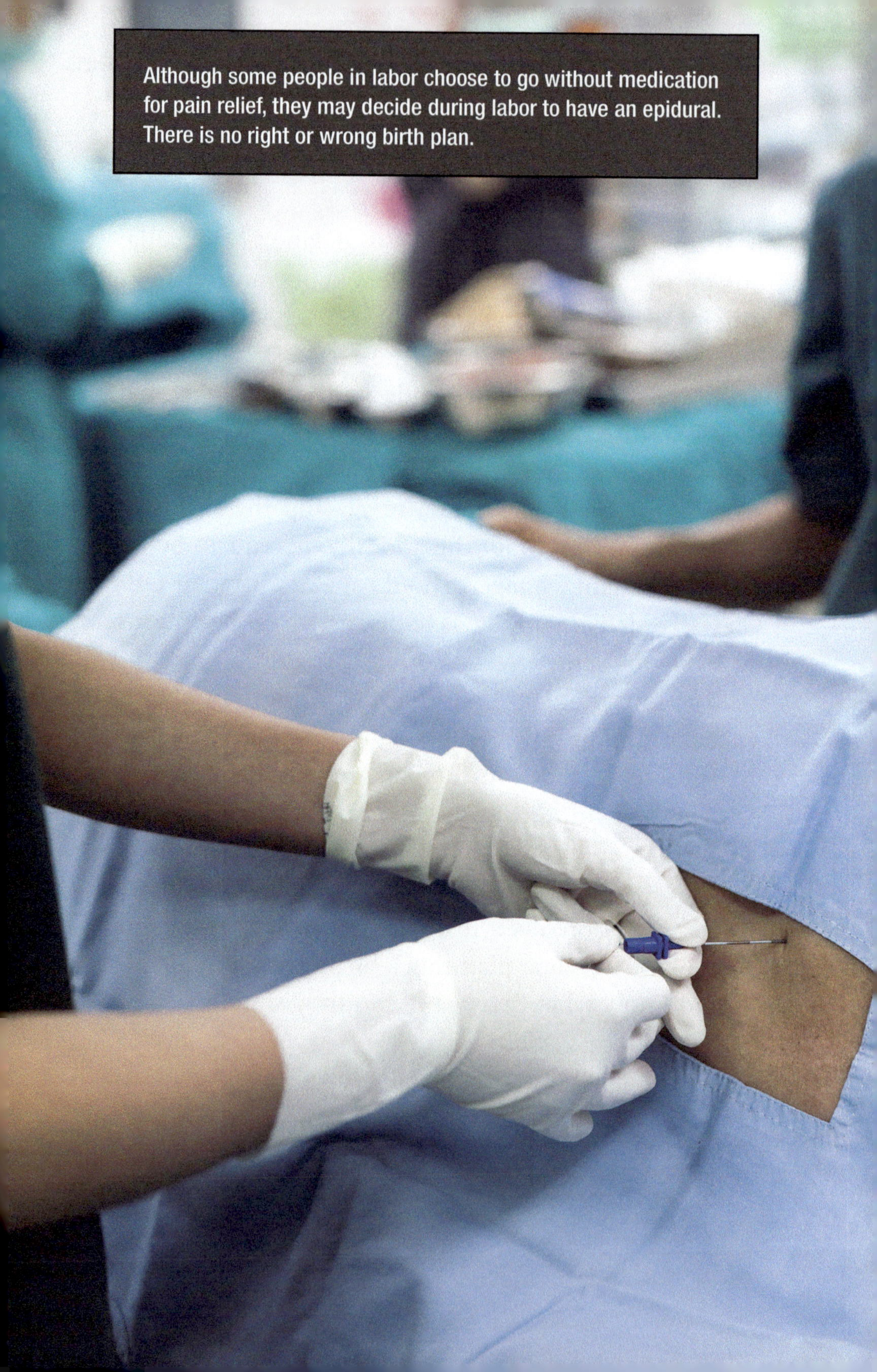

Although some people in labor choose to go without medication for pain relief, they may decide during labor to have an epidural. There is no right or wrong birth plan.

write this down. If she is giving birth to a boy, she'll also want to decide beforehand whether to have him circumcised (a procedure in which a doctor removes the foreskin of the penis). Globally, less than a third of all boys and men undergo this procedure. In some communities it is the cultural norm, but it is not a necessary procedure. Therefore, a parent will want to carefully consider what she prefers for her child.

Finally, a teenager will want to speak with all the professionals providing her with reproductive health care about her recovery and about birth control options for the future.

Feeding a Baby

There are a few options for feeding a baby: breastfeeding, formula, or a combination of both. Breastfeeding is the healthiest option for a baby, yet teenage mothers are less likely to breastfeed than mothers in any other demographic, according to multiple sources. Suzanne Najarian Goodson, an international board-certified lactation consultant

(continued on page 89)

Like all mothers, teenage mothers should be encouraged to breastfeed, and they should also be provided with information about breastfeeding.

(continued from page 87)

(IBCLC), believes that providing good information to teenagers about breastfeeding is important:

Najarian Goodson told the author:

> Teens face unique challenges to the choice to breastfeed, including being frequently discouraged to do so, feeling unsure how they will balance commitments and social activities with the time spent nursing the baby, and integrating this new way of viewing their body as nourishing their baby. These are counterbalanced by the rewards of increased confidence and strong bonding that accompany breastfeeding. Teen mothers, like any other, should be encouraged to breastfeed and provided with accurate information about breastfeeding, including pumping and bottle-feeding expressed milk when necessary or desirable.

However, breastfeeding doesn't work for everyone, and formula is a perfectly safe alternative. Ultimately, every new parent will make her own decision about how to feed her baby. Teenagers wanting to learn more about their options should speak with their doctors, midwives, doulas, or a lactation specialist. In addition, they may look up their local La Leche League chapter online to learn more information about breastfeeding.

Complications

Teenagers who carry their pregnancies to term are at higher risk of having health complications than women in older age demographics. According to the World Health Organization, complications from pregnancy and childbirth are the leading cause of death for girls between the ages of fifteen and nineteen around the world. In addition, social stigma can affect teenage mothers, and they are at greater risk for living in poverty. Knowing these risks can help teenagers watch for complications and discuss them with medical providers, social workers, and other professionals.

Health Risks to Teenage Parents and Their Children

Pregnant teenagers are at higher risk of having high blood pressure or of being anemic than older parents, and their children appear to have an increased risk of being born prematurely or of having low birth weight. Therefore, it's vital for teenagers to get proper prenatal care so

It's important that teenagers understand the risks of carrying a pregnancy to term so that they can make the right choices about their own bodies.

that a doctor can monitor their health and the health of their unborn children.

Teenagers are notorious for having unhealthy eating habits, but this doesn't need to be the case. Pregnant teens should adopt a nutritious diet and they should also take any prenatal vitamins their doctors recommend. It should go without saying that all pregnant people should stay physically active and should avoid smoking, alcohol, and other drugs.

Postpartum Depression

Like all people, teenagers may suffer from depression after giving birth. This depression usually appears within a couple months after giving birth. Signs that a new parent might be experiencing postpartum depression may include lacking a feeling of attachment to her baby, not wanting to take care of her baby, or isolating herself (either with or without her child).

Being a new parent is difficult, but a teenager's postpartum depression may stem from her economic situation, or she may be experiencing stigma from her family, classmates, or community. She may feel "stuck" and alone. Postpartum depression is a condition that must be addressed. Fortunately, there are plenty of people who can offer their support, including social workers, therapists, doctors, and teachers. In other words, a teenager's support network is often wider than she realizes.

Life After Pregnancy

Despite the stigma against teenage pregnancy and parenthood, there's no bad choice to make in regard to a pregnancy, so long as it's the choice of the pregnant person. Teenagers have a tremendous amount of legal power over the decisions they make regarding their reproductive health, including whether they choose to become parents.

Though pregnancy is a big deal, it doesn't define an adolescent. No matter whether a teenager decides to have an abortion or go through the entire process of pregnancy and childbirth in order to adopt out her baby or become a parent, there are many resources at her disposal, and she has a legal right to remain in school and even go on to college.

Although pregnant teenagers may feel shame due to the stigmatization of teenage pregnancy, it's important for them to know that they are neither bad people nor one-dimensional stereotypes. In fact, they are multidimensional human beings with the capacity to succeed wherever they set their sights.

10 Great Questions to Ask an OB/GYN or Midwife

1. What is your opinion of teenage mothers?
2. Will you respect my written birth plan?
3. If I have a doula, will you respect him or her as an advocate working on my behalf?
4. Who will deliver my baby?
5. Where will you deliver my baby?
6. How many babies have you delivered? How many each week?
7. Who will deliver my baby if you're not available?
8. What are your thoughts about pain management? What do you generally recommend?
9. Will all of the expenses of my labor and birth be covered by my insurance?
10. How often do you give C-sections, and why?

Glossary

abortion A medical procedure that ends a pregnancy.

adoption When a birth parent legally terminates her parental rights and places her child with another family.

birth control Also called family planning, birth control is a method used to prevent or plan pregnancy.

birth plan A set of instructions created by a pregnant person about her baby's birth. This plan may be made with a partner, but it is ultimately up to the pregnant person.

cisgender Description of people whose biological sex matches their gender identity.

consent Permission given to do something; often used in conversations about sex.

doula A person trained to provide emotional support to pregnant people during childbirth, as well as to families after a baby is born.

gender nonbinary A label for a person who does not identify as male or female.

judicial bypass A legal alternative for teens to obtain adoptions without parental notification or involvement.

midwife A medical professional trained to help with labor and delivery.

misogyny A hatred of women.

OB/GYN Short for obstetrician-gynecologist, an OB/GYN takes care of the reproductive health of people with female anatomy.

patriarchy A social system in which men hold the power.

reproduction The production of a baby, often through sex.

sex The label of male or female that is given to a person at birth by a medical professional, based on the person's anatomy.

stereotype An oversimplified belief or generalization, usually about a group of people.

stigma A feeling of disapproval or disgust that many people within a society have toward a group of people or an idea.

transgender Description of people whose biologically assigned sex doesn't match their gender identity.

American Civil Liberties Union (ACLU)
125 Broad Street, 18th Floor
New York, NY 10004
Website: https://www.aclu.org
Facebook and Twitter: @aclu
Instagram: @aclu_nationwide
The ACLU is a national organization that defends people's civil liberties in courts, legislatures, and communities across the country.

GED Testing Service (joint venture of the American Council on Education and Pearson VUE)
1919 M Street NW, Suite 600
Washington, DC 20036
(877) 392-6433
Website: https://www.gedtestingservice.com/educators/current-testing-program
Facebook and Twitter: @GEDTesting
Instagram: @my_ged
The GED Testing Service is a nationally recognized high school equivalency program that enables people without high school diplomas to continue their education.

Planned Parenthood Federation of America
1110 Vermont Avenue NW
Washington, DC 20005
(800) 230-7526

Website: https://www.plannedparenthood.org
Facebook and Instagram: @plannedparenthood
Twitter: @PPFA
Planned Parenthood is a national organization with over six hundred health centers offering services from STD treatments, cancer screenings, prenatal care, birth control, and abortions.

Public Health Agency of Canada
130 Colonnade Road
AL 6501H
Ottawa, ON K1A 0K9
Canada
(844) 280-5020
Website: https://www.canada.ca/en/public-health.html
Facebook: @Public-Health-Agency-of-Canada
Twitter: @PHAC_GC
This agency of the Canadian government provides a wealth of information and resources on all areas of health and wellness, including information to support informed decision making regarding pregnancy and childbirth.

Rape, Abuse & Incest National Network (RAINN) & the National Sexual Assault Hotline
2000 L Street NW, Suite 406
Washington, DC 20036

(800) 656-HOPE (4673)
Website: https://www.rainn.org
Facebook: @RAINN01
Instagram and Twitter: @RAINN
RAINN is the largest sexual violence prevention organization in the United States and provides a hotline and chat services for victims and survivors of sexual violence. Staff can connect you with providers in your area.

SexEd
Website: http://sexedproject.org
Email: liz@sexedproject.org
Facebook: @S3x3dproject
SexEd is an "art-inspired community-based" sex education program. It aims to destigmatize sex, raise awareness about consent, and facilitate open conversations around topics of sex and sexuality.

US Department of Education: Office for Civil Rights & Title IX and Sex Discrimination
400 Maryland Avenue SW
Washington, DC 20202
(800) 872-5327
Website: https://www2.ed.gov
Facebook: @ED.gov
Instagram and Twitter: @usedgov

This office of the US government enforces Title IX, which protects people from discrimination based on sex and upholds the rights of pregnant people to education.

US Department of Health and Human Services: Medicare and Medicaid Services
7500 Security Boulevard
Woodlawn, MD 21244
(877) 267-2323
Website: https://www.medicaid.gov
Facebook: @Centers-for-Medicare-and-Medicaid-Services
Twitter: @MedicaidGov
The Medicaid website provides information about how to apply for Medicaid coverage and the Children's Health Insurance Program (CHIP).

For Further Reading

Angier, Natalie. *Women: An Intimate Geography.* Boston, MA: Houghton Mifflin Harcourt, 1999.

Benson, Alana. *Everything You Need to Know About Birth Control.* New York, NY: Rosen Publishing, 2019.

Corinna, Heather. *S.E.X.: The All-You-Need-To-Know Sexuality Guide to Get You Through Your Teens and Twenties.* Boston, MA: Da Capo Lifelong Books, 2016.

DeCarlo, Carolyn. *Everything You Need to Know About the Risks of Unprotected Sex.* New York, NY: Rosen Publishing, 2019.

Fonda, Jane. *Being a Teen: Everything Teen Girls and Boys Should Know About Relationships, Sex, Love, Health, Identity & More.* New York, NY: Random House Trade Paperbacks, 2014.

Henderson, Elisabeth, and Nancy Armstrong. *100 Questions You'd Never Ask Your Parents: Straight Answers to Teens' Questions About Sex, Sexuality, and Health.* New York, NY: Roaring Brook Press, 2013.

Kamberg, Mary-Lane. *Teen Pregnancy and Motherhood.* New York, NY: Rosen Publishing, 2013.

Koya, Lena. *Teen Pregnancy and What Comes Next* (Women in the World). New York, NY: Rosen Publishing, 2018.

Mayer, Melissa. *Coping with Date Rape and Acquaintance Rape*. New York, NY: Rosen Publishing, 2019.

Murkoff, Heidi. *What to Expect When You're Expecting*. New York, NY: Workman Publishing Company, 2016.

Norsigian, Judy, and Boston Women's Health Book Collective. *Our Bodies, Our Selves*. New York, NY: Touchstone Publishing, 2005.

Rodriguez, Gaby. *The Pregnancy Project: A Memoir*. New York, NY: Simon & Schuster Books for Young Readers, 2013.

Bibliography

Buchanan, Christy. "Mothers' Generalized Beliefs About Adolescents: Links to Expectations for a Specific child." *Journal of Research on Adolescence* 23, no. 1 (February 2003). http://journals.sagepub.com/doi/abs/10.1177/0272431602239129.

Centers for Disease Control and Prevention. "Teen Pregnancy in the United States." About Teen Pregnancy. May 9, 2017. https://www.cdc.gov/teenpregnancy/about/index.htm.

Chambers, Brittany D., and Jennifer Toller Erausquin. "The Promise of Intersectional Stigma to Understand the Complexities of Adolescent Pregnancy and Motherhood." *Journal of Child and Adolescent Behavior* 3, no. 249 (October 9, 2015).

FBI: The Uniform Crime Reporting (UCR) Program. "Rape." Retrieved February 15, 2018. https://ucr.fbi.gov/crime-in-the-u.s/2013/crime-in-the-u.s.-2013/violent-crime/rape.

Guttmacher Institute. "Adolescent Sexual and Reproductive Health in the United States." September 2017. https://www.guttmacher.org/fact-sheet/american-teens-sexual-and-reproductive-health.

Interview with Kim Jorgensen Gane, Leadership Council for Planned Parenthood's National Speaker Bureau. Brooklyn, NY. April 5, 2018.

Interview with Rose Tell-Drake, parent. Brooklyn, NY. April 5, 2018.

Interview with Suzanne Najarian Goodson, IBCLC (international board-certified lactation consultant). Brooklyn, NY. April 6, 2018.

Lindley, Lisa L., and Katrina M. Walsemann. "Sexual Orientation and Risk of Pregnancy Among New York City High-School Students." *American Journal of Public Health* 105, no. 7 (July 1, 2015): 1379–1386.

McClendon, David, and Aleksandra Sandstrom. "Child Marriage Is Rare in the US, Though This Varies by State." Pew Research Center. Retrieved March 20, 2018. http://www.pewresearch.org/fact-tank/2016/11/01/child-marriage-is-rare-in-the-u-s-though-this-varies-by-state.

National Academies of Sciences, Engineering, and Medicine. "The Safety and Quality of Abortion Care in the United States." March 16, 2018. https://www.nap.edu/read/24950/chapter/1#ii.

National Committee for Adoption. *Adoption Factbook: United States Data, Issues, Regulations and Resources.* Washington, DC: National Committee for Adoption, 1989.

Orlando Women's Center. "Abortion Facts Around the World." Retrieved March 15, 2018. http://www.womenscenter.com/abortion_stats.html.

Planned Parenthood. "Abortion After the First Trimester in the United States." February 2014. https://www.plannedparenthood.org/files/5113/9611/5527/Abortion_After_first_trimester.pdf.

Planned Parenthood. "All About Sex." Retrieved March 6, 2018. https://www.plannedparenthood.org/learn/teens/sex/all-about-sex.

RAINN. "Children and Teens: Statistics." Retrieved March 1, 2018. https://www.rainn.org/statistics/children-and-teens.

RAINN. "Victims of Sexual Violence: Statistics." Retrieved March 1, 2018. https://www.rainn.org/statistics/victims-sexual-violence.

Raymond, Elizabeth G., and David A. Grimes. "The Comparative Safety of Legal Induced Abortion and Childbirth in the United States." *Obstetrics & Gynecology* 119, no. 2 (February 2012): 215–219.

Rocca, Corinne H., et al. "Decision Rightness and Emotional Responses to Abortion in the United States: A Longitudinal Study." *PLOS One* (July 8, 2015). http://journals.plos.org/plosone/article?id=10.1371/journal.pone.0128832.

Society for Adolescent Health and Medicine. "Abstinence-Only-Until-Marriage Policies and Programs: An Updated Position Paper of the Society for Adolescent Health and Medicine." 61, no. 3 (September 2017): 400–403.

Stanger-Hall, Kathrin, and David Hall. "Abstinence-Only Education and Teen Pregnancy Rates: Why We Need Comprehensive Sex Education in the U.S." *PLOS One* (October 14, 2011). https://www.ncbi.nlm.nih.gov/pmc/articles/PMC3194801.

Thompson, Kirsten M. J. "A Brief History of Birth Control in the U.S." Our Bodies Ourselves, December 14, 2013. https://www.ourbodiesourselves.org/health-info/a-brief-history-of-birth-control.

Thompson, Kirsten M. J. "Why Birth Control Is Essential to Women Everywhere." Our Bodies Ourselves, December 14, 2013. https://www.ourbodiesourselves.org/health-info/why-birth-control-is-essential-to-women-everywhere.

Thompson, Sanna J., et al. "Runaway and Pregnant: Risk Factors Associated with Pregnancy in a National Sample of Runaway/Homeless Female Adolescents." *Journal of Adolescent Health* 43, no. 2 (August 2008): 125–132. https://www.ncbi.nlm.nih.gov/pmc/articles/PMC2742657.

United Nations Population Fund (UNFPA). "Reproductive Rights are Human Rights: A Handbook for National Human Rights Institutions." 2014. https://www.unfpa.org/publications/reproductive-rights-are-human-rights.

Upadhyay, Ushma D., et al. "Incidence of Emergency Department Visits and Complications After Abortion." *Obstetrics & Gynecology* 125, no. 1: 175–183. January 2015.

US Department of Health and Human Services. "Trends in Teen Pregnancy and Childbearing." Retrieved February 15, 2018. https://www.hhs.gov/ash/oah/adolescent-development/reproductive-health-and-teen-pregnancy/teen-pregnancy-and-childbearing/trends/index.html.

World Health Organization. "Adolescent Pregnancy: Fact Sheet." Updated January 2018. http://www.who.int/mediacentre/factsheets/fs364/en.

Index

About the Author

Melissa Banigan is the founder and CEO of Advice Project Media, a nonprofit organization that offers journalism and travel services for teens, youth, and women around the world. An author and educator, she has taught and lectured about gender equality, feminism, and teen rights in the United States, Cameroon, Peru, and Guadeloupe. Also a journalist, Banigan has bylines in many national and international publications, including the Washington Post, CNN, NPR, and the BBC.

Photo Credits

Cover BananaStock/Thinkstock; p. 5 Jason LaVeris/FilmMagic /Getty Images; p. 9 Pixelheadphoto digitalskillet/Shutterstock.com; p. 13 Jim Craigmyle/Corbis/Getty Images; pp. 16–17 © iStockphoto.com /Jetcityimage; p. 19 Mr. Zach/Shutterstock.com; p. 22 Garo/Phanie /Passage/Getty Images; p. 29 Antoniodiaz/Shutterstock.com; pp. 32–33 Stephane De Sakutin/AFP/Getty Images; p. 34 SW Productions /Photodisc/Getty Images; pp. 38–39 Monkey Business Images /Shutterstock.com; p. 41 © AP Images; pp. 44–45 Brendan Smialowski /AFP/Getty Images; p. 46 Brigette Supernova/Alamy Stock Photo; p. 51 Rena Schild/Shutterstock.com; p. 53 Design Pics/Colleen Cahill /Getty Images; p. 58 Ian Hooton/Science Photo Library/Getty Images; pp. 60–61 KPG Ivary/Shutterstock.com; p. 64 Tony Anderson /Digital Vision/Getty Images; p. 67 Asiseeit/E+/Getty Images; p. 70 JGA/Shutterstock.com; pp. 72–73 designer491/Alamy Stock Photo; p. 77 Lev Malevich/Shutterstock.com; p. 79 Andrey Popov /Shutterstock.com; pp. 82–83 James Davies/Alamy Stock Photo; p. 86 ChaNaWit/Shutterstock.com; pp. 88–89 LWA/Dann Tardif /Blend Images/Getty Images; pp. 90–91 globalmoments /Shutterstock.com.

Design and Layout: Nicole Russo-Duca; Editor: Rachel Aimee; Photo Researcher: Sherri Jackson